MY NAME IS
RACHEL CORRIE

Rachel Corrie was born in Olympia, Washington, on April 10th, 1979. Before completing her studies at The Evergreen State College in Olympia she joined other foreign nationals working for the International Solidarity Movement in Gaza on January 25th, 2003. This text has been edited from her journals and e-mails.

MY NAME IS RACHEL CORRIE

Taken from the Writings of Rachel Corrie

Edited by Alan Rickman and Katharine Viner

With kind permission of the Corrie family

*In collaboration with
the Royal Court Theatre International Department*

THEATRE COMMUNICATIONS GROUP
NEW YORK
2006

My Name Is Rachel Corrie is published by Theatre Communications Group, Inc., 520 Eighth Avenue, 24th Floor, New York, NY 10018-4156, by special arrangement with Nick Hern Books Limited.

First published in Great Britain as a paperback original in 2005 by Nick Hern Books, in association with the Royal Court Theatre, London.

A CIP catalog record for this book is available from the Library of Congress.

ISBN-13: 978-1-55936-296-2
ISBN-10: 1-55936-296-0

TCG books are exclusively distributed to the book trade by Consortium Book Sales and Distribution.

Cover image: Rachel Corrie at Mima Mounds, Washington, courtesy of the Corrie family.

First TCG Edition, May 2006
Third Printing, August 2009

MY NAME IS
RACHEL CORRIE

My Name Is Rachel Corrie was first presented at the Royal Court Theatre, London, on April 7, 2005. It was revived at the Royal Court Theatre in October 2005. It transferred to the Playhouse Theatre in London's West End in March 2006 (produced by David Johnson and Virginia Buckley). It was first produced in the U.S. at the Minetta Lane Theater in New York City, in October 2006 (produced by Dena Hammerstein and Pam Pariseau for James Hammerstein Productions).

Performed by Megan Dodds
Directed by Alan Rickman
Designed by Hildegard Bechtler
Lighting designed by Johanna Town
Sound and Video designed by Emma Laxton
Associate Director, Tiffany Watt-Smith

For the Royal Court Theatre:
Artistic Director, Ian Rickson
Associate Director International, Elyse Dodgson
International Administrator, Chris James
General Manager, Diane Borger
Production Managers, Sue Bird and Paul Handley

The Royal Court would like to thank the following for their help: Nicholas Blincoe; Alice Coy; David Crampton and the Evergreen State College, Olympia; Tom Dale; Nick Durie; Uri Fruchtmann; Mohammed Qeshta; Jeff Halper; David Hare; Jenny; Sandra Jordan; Jonah Lotan; Helena Meyer-Knapp; Anna Paterson; Linda Ramsden; Lucy Record; Jacqueline Rose and Susi Wooldridge.

Olympia, Washington. A bedroom. Clothes, books everywhere.
RACHEL *lies on top of it all.*

Every morning I wake up in my red bedroom that seemed like
genius when I painted it, but looks more and more like carnage
these days. I blink for a minute. I get ready to write down some
dreams or a page in my diary or draw some very important
maps. And then the ceiling tries to devour me.

I wriggle around under my comforter trying to find a ball
point, a Crayola, anything fast. I can hear the ceiling spit and
gnash above me. Waiting for me to look, because if I look, it
can eat me.

And I struggle for some socks and some boxers so I can make
a run for it – but I haven't done laundry in a month and the
other girl who lives in my room when I'm not here – the bad
one who tends the garden of dirty cups and throws all the
clothes around and tips over the ashtrays – the bad other girl
hid all my pens while I was sleeping.

And I try. I try to look at my fingers. I try to look at the floor
with all the fashion magazines left by the bad other girl, to find
one pen – just one pen. But I can't imagine where any pens
might be, and trying to imagine, I get off guard for a minute
and my eyes roll up towards the sky and I'm fucked now – I'm
fucked – 'cause there is no sky. There's that ceiling up there
and it has me now – 'cause I'm looking at it and it's going to
rip me to pieces.

She sits and faces us.

I am a creator of intricately decorated bedrooms. Each time
I move, I spend weeks painting, gluing things to my walls,
choosing the precise pictures of goddesses and art postcards.
This is a labour of love, and I become completely immersed
in it.

I wonder why I didn't notice the awfulness of my room before.
I am inside a terrifying mirror.

I glued things to the wall. My God, I glued things to my wall.

Touching the pictures, picking up books.

The question is always where to start the story. That's the first
question. Trying to find a beginning, trying to impose order on
the great psychotic fast-forward merry-go-round, and trying to
impose order is the first step toward ending up in a park
somewhere, painted blue, singing 'Row, row, row your boat' to
an audience of saggy-lipped junkies and business people
munching oat-bran muffins.

And that's how this story ends, good buddy, so if you are
concerned with the logic and sequence of things and the
crescendo of suspense up to a good shocker of an ending, you
best be getting back to your video game and your amassing
wealth. Leave the meaningless details to the poets and the
photographers.

And they're all meaningless details, my friend.

She finds a journal and turns the pages.

1991.

My name is Rachel Corrie. I am twelve years old. I was born on April 10th, 1979 in Olympia, Washington, to my mother and father, Craig and Cindy Corrie, a brother, Chris, a sister, Sarah, and a really old cat named Phoebe.

I grew. I learned to spell cat, to read little books. When I was five I discovered boys, which made my life a little more difficult. Just a little, and a lot more interesting.

In second grade there were classroom rules hanging from the ceiling. The only one I can remember now seems like it would be a good rule for life. 'Everyone must feel safe.' Safe to be themselves, physically safe, safe to say what they think, just safe. That's the best rule I can think of.

Now I'm in middle school. I guess I've grown up a little, it's all relative anyway, nine years is as long as forty years depending on how long you've lived. I stole that from my dad.

Sometimes I think my dad is the wisest person in the world.

You understand none of this is really true, because what I wrote today is true, but you'll read it by tomorrow, or the next day, and my whole life will be different. Is that how life is, a new draft for every day, a new view for each hour?

When I graduated fifth grade we had a list of questions for our yearbook. One of them was 'What do you want to be when you grow up?' Everyone wrote something like 'doctor' or 'astronaut' or 'Spiderman,' and then you turned the page and there was my five-paragraph manifesto on the million things I wanted to be, from wandering poet to first woman president. That was real cute in fifth grade but when it's ten years later, I'm a junior in college, and I still don't have the conviction to cross 'Spiderman' off my list – well, you can imagine it gets a little nerve-wracking.

My mother used to walk with me to the bottom of the hill to wait for the car pool – I was nervous that I would do it wrong. I remember, or maybe I invent, that occasionally we decided on the way, I wasn't going to school. We stole time that way. She took me to lunch. We went to bookstores in Seattle. She bought me books on love and delinquency, and although she never said it straight out, I'm sure she was hoping I'd become a bank robber. My mother would never admit it, but she wanted me exactly how I turned out – scattered and deviant and too loud.

She changes her clothes.

I'm building the world myself and putting new hats on everybody one by one, before I go out, so wrinkled, I have to grab the great big flaccid flaps of my eyebrows and lift them off my cheekbones in order to see. Before I go out I'm gonna have people in tutus, cops wearing sombreros, stockbrokers with Viking hats, priests with panties on their heads. In the world I'm building, everybody shouts hello to everybody else from their car windows. People have speakers attached to their chests that pour out music so you can tell from a distance what mood they're in, and they won't be too chicken to get naked when the rain comes. And first ladies carry handcuffs and bull whips and presidents wear metal collars. Big metal collars with tight leashes.

She emerges. Barefoot.

Okay. I'm Rachel. Sometimes I wear ripped blue jeans.
Sometimes I wear polyester. Sometimes I take off all my
clothes and swim naked at the beach. I don't believe in fate but
my astrological sign is Aries, the ram, and my sign on the
Chinese zodiac is the sheep, and the name Rachel means sheep
but I've got a fire in my belly. It used to be such a big loud
blazing fire that I couldn't hear anybody else over it. So I talked
a lot and I didn't listen too much. Then I went to middle school
where you gotta be *cool* and you gotta be *strong* and *tough*,
and I tried real hard to be cool. But luckily, luckily I happened
to get a free trip to Russia and I saw another country for the
first time.

In the streets and the alleys it was an obstacle course of garbage
and mud and graffiti. There was coal dust on the snow,
everything was dirty. And they always said to us, 'How do
you like our dirty city?' Oh, but it was so pretty with the little
lights in the windows and the red dusk-light on the buildings.
It was flawed, dirty, broken and gorgeous.

I looked backwards across the Pacific Ocean and from that
distance some things back here in Olympia, Washington, USA
seemed a little weird and disconcerting. But I was awake in
Russia. I was awake for the first time with bug-eyes and a grin.

On the flight home from Anchorage to Seattle everything was
dark. Then the sun began to rise, the water was shining, and
I realized we were flying over Puget Sound. Soon we could see
islands in that water, evergreen trees on those islands.

And I began to sob. I sobbed in all that radiance, in the midst
of the most glorious sunrise I'd ever seen, because it wasn't
enough. It wasn't enough to make me glad to be home.

Maybe it was finally the trees who told me to stay. Or maybe
going to school in my hometown was just the path of least
resistance. Maybe going to Evergreen State College was just
the best way to be different from my Economics-major-high
achiever-khaki-and-high-heels-Yalie-corporate sister and
brother. I don't know why I stayed. But one day I knew I had
to. It was the same day I decided to be an artist and a writer

and I didn't give a shit if I was mediocre and I didn't give a shit if I starved to death and I didn't give a shit if my whole damn high school turned and pointed and laughed in my face.

I was finally awake, forever and ever.

Picking up a print-out.

Yesterday I heard from Chris in Gaza. I am being invited there. I need to go.

I've been organizing in Olympia for a little over a year on anti-war/global justice issues. And it started to feel like this work is missing a connection to the people who are impacted by US foreign policy. I just think we all have the right to be critical of government policies . . . any government policies, particularly policies which we're funding. I feel pretty isolated from the world because of living in Olympia my whole life and my activism at this point has been extremely tied to Olympia. But I've had this underlying need to go to a place and meet people who are on the other end of the tax money that goes to fund the US military. Trying to be local and be respectful of the local is a big part of my ethic, I guess.

What I need to do.

She writes in her notebook.

Send Tuesday's minutes out over the internet.
Write an article for Monday's staff newsletter.
Call Tom again.
Make a list of things hanging over my head.

I am given to making very important lists.

Reading from her notebook.

Five People I Wish I'd Met Who Are Dead:
Salvador Dali
Karl Jung
MLK
JFK
Josephine.

Five People To Hang Out With In Eternity:
Rainer Maria Rilke
Jesus
ee cummings
Gertrude Stein
Zelda Fitzgerald

Six – Charlie Chaplin.

She starts to pack a bag.

I didn't intend to become so deeply involved in activism this year. I'm not sure what compelled me to sign up for the Local Knowledge class – there's such a big degree of community involvement. I'm phobic of community. I'm scared of people, particularly people in the greater Olympia area.

I've been here my whole life. Almost everyone I know and have known in Olympia came from somewhere else.

This is another place where progressive white people escaped a few decades ago – a place where hippie kids come after touring with jam bands.

I don't think my intention was to be of any particular use to the communities we studied. I was looking for curious facts to flesh out an authentic setting. Trivia.

Like – when I worked at Mount Rainier we followed a woman into the woods. She had become part owl. Her job was to entice them out. Our job was to carry the live mice. Somehow, after years of doing spotted owl survey, this woman's larynx changed. She croaked in a language that was articulated somewhere deeper than tonsils. Her tongue must have changed shape. We followed her through the woods on the northwest side of the mountain all day and we saw no owls. And no owls croaked back at her.

I think about how many of us doing any kind of progressive work in this region swim beneath the surface combing for what was here before, and taking inventory of what is now. There's the chance that you will be changed by what you're looking for. Your tongue could change shape like the woman at Rainier.

Studying the history of this area roots me. We've certainly waded in the same water and wandered on the same beaches as very brave people. It makes bravery seem more possible.

We can look at that history and then choose which side we want to be on now, and how willing we are to fight. We are not outside.

Over a thousand people are still, as far as I can tell, being held somewhere in the United States, and it's unclear why. They arrest the 'dirty-bomber,' someone apparently 'in the very early stages' of planning an attack on the US, and this is big news. What does this say about the other thousand people held somewhere? That they weren't in the early stages of planning anything.

Looking for where I fit into all this forced me out into the community.

You come to take for granted where you belong in a town. If you have an overactive fantasy life you just start making things up. You can remember just enough unrelated pieces of trivia to hold up coffee-table conversation and never have to think about anything disturbing or demanding of action.

I'm still pretty shell-shocked by this semester. I spoke to a room of about forty international students. I've helped in the planning of two conferences, facilitated meetings, danced down the street with forty people from the ages of seven to seventy, dressed as doves. I spent a lot of time with the homeless group. I went with them to the city council. I went to the community conversation. I slept out overnight on Mayday.

Who is this person? How did I get here?

I will not leave the house if it's to turn in my own work or complete some other act of self-preservation. I will never leave my bed.

The salmon talked me into a lifestyle change. There's a hole, a pipe, in the bulkhead at the East Bay Marina. Every year salmon swim into that hole, trying to get back home. Salmon have to make it all the way up Plum Street in that hole. That hole is Moxlie Creek.

Once you know that there are salmon down there it's hard to forget. You imagine their moony eyes while you walk home from the bar in your slutty boots. It's hard to be extraordinarily vacuous when you always have the salmon in the back of your mind: in that pipe down there – on their way to daylight at Watershed Park. Salmon are the history that isn't trivia. They are what was here before.

I look at this place now and I just want to do right by it. The salmon beneath downtown and the creeks and the inlets and the people who were here first and my elementary school teachers and my mom.

Leaving a phone message.

Hey Mom, could you e-mail to me with anyone you know who it would be good to contact if I get in trouble – though I'm not planning on it – friends or family who would call their Congress people, etc. – also, friends who might be interested in getting info or at least knowing that I'm going?

I'm going to give *The Olympian* your number. Please think about your language when you talk to them. I think it was smart that you're wary of using the word 'terrorism', and if you talk about the cycle of violence, or 'an eye for an eye', you could be perpetuating the idea that the Israeli-Palestinian conflict is a balanced conflict, instead of a largely unarmed people against the fourth most powerful military in the world. These are the kind of things it's important to think about before talking to reporters.

I'll call you tonight.

We have a very involved mother . . . overly involved sometimes. This means we have to claw our way toward autonomy – kick and scream and yell to get some space to grow in. It also means we let her take care of things we are capable of doing ourselves.

I think of my mom as being extremely moralistic. Not in a bad way. Just there were things that none of us did. Lying, teasing, taking things, just being rude to people. Sometimes she wondered if we would be healthier, better children if she had taken us to church. This may have been a scare tactic of hers.

I know a woman who's pregnant and she's decided not to assign a gender to her baby until it chooses its own. I think that's a little nuts. Anyway, I think maybe my mom had a similar attitude toward my spirituality. She was determined I would define it for myself.

I could write a history of my family according to discoveries I've made over the years in cupboards and drawers. Unfinished baby books. Duplicate containers of oregano from houses I lived in and moved out of, taking the seasoning with me. Placemats that defeated cranberry juice and oyster stew and candle wax.

I am heartbroken when I search in my mother's drawers. I am heartbroken by the way she arranges jewelery. I know she returns her earrings to their little boxes when she finishes with them. I am heartbroken at the thought of her, standing in her big bra and her pantyhose stretched over her underwear, dabbing on lipstick, moving pink powder across the bones of her cheeks, rubbing it into her pores until it hangs on. My mother ages and puts on make-up – slides bracelets across her wrists – where the skin is loose.

Sometimes my mother is up there, bobbing in the sky like Macy's Parade balloons. Sometimes my mother is so big she looms over everything.

Finding a photograph of Cindy, her mother.

I know I scare you, Mom.

I'm sorry I scare you. But I want to write and I want to see.
And what would I write about if I only stayed within the doll's
house, the flower-world I grew up in?

You gave me a potential.

I love you but I'm growing out of what you gave me. I'm
saving it inside me and growing outwards. Let me fight my
monsters. You made me. You made me.

Packing photograph of Cindy.

Mom, why doesn't Dad ever write to me? Has he gotten
himself addicted to cocaine while he's away and forgotten
about his family? He never wrote back to me and gave me
fatherly advice about how to get a job . . . or told me how he
almost got swept into the ocean looking for whelks. If this
continues I'm going to have to start dating 40-year-old men to
make up for my underdeveloped animus.

Actually, Dad, that was just a little joke, but I think it is
important that I fill you in on some sketchy things that have
been going on up here. Don't tell Mom who tipped you off, but
the mailman's been coming by a lot more than usual, and
staying for a real long time, and wearing really racy high-cut
mailman shorts. And Mom's been dressing real trampy. I just
thought you should know.

RACHEL *as Craig, her father.*

'You're just like your mother. Making fun of people with
disabilities. You criticize me for not writing when I can hardly
see the computer, let alone the type on its screen. Now that I

have reading glasses, my wife says they make my eyes look too big. Yet I understand your criticism. I should have written you, sighted or not, it's no excuse. Never mind that all I get is the hand-me-downs. The cast-off e-mails written to your mother that she may choose to share with her husband. Or not. But I don't complain. It's a father's life: work all day so that others may enjoy. I give it freely. Never a word from me!'

RACHEL *to Craig.*

You never get your own personal e-mails because if I so much as give you a 'heads up' in one of my e-mails to Mom, I have to prepare myself for the mockery and neo-liberal jabs at my progressive education that are always the thanks I get. Down, oppressor man!

To the audience.

Incidentally, at this point, the neo-liberal jabs are pretty close to the mark. At one lecture, our guest speaker was, I think, a physicist. But his side occupation is dream-work. 'Hi, my name is Dr Jenson, I'm a Harvard grad with a PhD in Political Economy, but on the side I analyze the paintings of my pet donkey, Aphrodite.'

I like my class. The reading is very interesting. The schedule is completely indecipherable. And the teachers wrap themselves in paper, sing in German, and yell insults at us to help us get a grasp on Dadaism.

To Craig.

It's a good thing that you, Chris and Sarah all appear to have stable salaries, because I am steadfastly pursuing a track that guarantees I'll never get paid more than three Triscuits and some spinach.

RACHEL *packs Craig's photograph.*

Packing away bed, books, etc.

What I have –
a house cat.
small hands, crooked toes, knees, elbows
thighs, a throat and a belly.
dirt under my nails.
six lost journals underneath seats
in trains across the country
a Buick. questionable.
eight black ballpoint pens
sharp teeth
beady eyes
and hope.

What I want –
a garden with pumpkins
and bare earth to turn over and
turn over
hardwood floors for sock ballets
air and raspberries
sometimes in the morning
danger and stolen kisses
from a sneaky mystery lover man.

Picking up a photograph of Colin.

I have exactly as much of Colin's memory as I need. The sun
was shining, Colin read political economy in the green chair.
I danced around to Magnetic Fields and mowed the lawn.

We walked to school together in the morning, and finally it
rained. Colin wanted me to walk faster. Colin always wanted to
walk faster, and I wanted to trudge and identify ferns.

I woke up early one day with errands to run and decided I would bump into Colin and his new hoochie-ass girlfriend. I shaved my armpits. I danced around in front of the mirror in the tight shirt I got in the little boy's section of the Salvation Army. I smeared on ChapStick.

'Fun life,' I say, 'Fun life.' I imagine I live in a Mountain Dew commercial. I am always on the beach with a bevy of sinewed friends and we're always dancing.

I meander through downtown. They are here somewhere, most likely in a shadow, ensnared together. They'll drop the spoons in their strawberry milkshake when I slide past. Free as a bird. Fun life. Toucan Sam.

They are not at the coffee shop. They are not in the grocery store, on the bridge, at the magazine stand. I drive to the school, embarrassed at myself. Of course he emerges from the library. Minus hoochie-ass girlfriend. I shove my hips out in the sun and make six-guns. He makes six-guns back at me. This town ain't big enough for the two of us.

'Hey-hey.'

'Hey-hey.'

'What are you doing here?'

'Reading up on some young anarchists.'

He pronounces his words like rubber bands stretched and snapping. I perform a dance beneath the conversation, like I have to pee.

Fun life. Fun life. Fun life.

'How are you?'

He's uncomfortable. I grin, sunshine on the apples of my cheeks.

'Well. I'm well. Meeting some people.'

I'm always on the beach with a bevy of sinewed friends.

'How are you?'

'Good. Gotta job scrubbing toilets.'

'Nice!'

'My friend from North Carolina went home.'

'You had a friend here from North Carolina?'

'You know – Leslie.'

Sunshine on the apples of my cheeks, sticky in my eyelashes and I'm on the beach and I'm always dancing.

'Shit, Colin! What happened? But things were going so well!'

He shook his head. Laughed at me.

It is easy to make the journey. You will know when the time comes. You will fall in love with someone who is perpetually leaving you. Someone who beats you at Scrabble and talks with big words and tells all stories as if they are blues songs. You will memorize the features of someone whose eyes are perpetually bored and whose lips are perpetually amused.

Eventually, I convinced Colin to quit drowning out my life. The topography of his life consisted of emergency adrenaline shots, jail, sometimes near-death experiences. The topography of my life consisted of making up names for the neighborhood cats, on some days a small new poem, the gossip among my friends. His life was skyscrapers. My life took place on a much smaller scale. That is done now. We are proportionate.

Putting on her shoes and socks.

On Wednesday I walked into the forest. Down the path to the little wooden bridge over the creek. And I stood on the bridge and looked at a log that lay across the little stream. Someone had taken rocks from the stream and lined them up like little multicolored frogs across the log.

I took off my boots and my socks and set them down on the edge of the bridge. Then I jumped onto the bank and climbed onto that log and walked across it, barefoot, nimbly, so that only one of the rocks fell into the water. I squatted in the pebbles and fished interesting rocks out of the stream for myself. I cleaned them and held them and put them in my pocket. Then I stood like Huck Finn with my jeans rolled up, with my back to the bridge and my two empty little brown boots. I sang to the forest. I hummed. I made up waltzes. I belted out Russian drinking songs. Opened my mouth wide and sang.

She sings.

Leaving Olympia.

We are all born and someday we'll all die. Most likely to some degree alone.

What if our aloneness isn't a tragedy? What if our aloneness is what allows us to speak the truth without being afraid? What if our aloneness is what allows us to adventure – to experience the world as a dynamic presence – as a changeable, interactive thing?

If I lived in Bosnia or Rwanda or who knows where else, needless death wouldn't be a distant symbol to me, it wouldn't be a metaphor, it would be a reality.

And I have no right to this metaphor. But I use it to console myself. To give a fraction of meaning to something enormous and needless.

This realization. This realization that I will live my life in this world where I have privileges.

I can't cool boiling waters in Russia. I can't be Picasso. I can't be Jesus. I can't save the planet single-handedly.

I can wash dishes.

Arriving in Jerusalem.

January 25th, 2003.

Very little problem at the airport. My tight jeans and cropped
bunny-hair sweater seem to have made all the difference – and
of course the use of my Israeli friend's address. The only
question was, 'Where did you meet her?' The woman behind
the glass appeared not to notice my shaking hands. I took a
shared taxi into Jerusalem and noticed that the Holy Land is
full of rocks and it seems like driving, you could fall off these
hills. Just before we leave the airport I read, in the *Let's Go
Israel* book, that more Israelis have been killed in car accidents
than in all of Israel's wars combined. I'm still trying to decide
what to make of this tidbit of information a day later.

Writing in notebook.

Things to do:
Buy phone card
Buy phone
E-mail Michael
Call Joe & Gili
Change money
Call Mom with cell number.

My introduction to curfew was gentle: a rush outside in the
midst of our training to buy lunch before the shops closed in
Beit Sahour. There was music – singing in Arabic – pouring
into the street from somewhere. By the time the whole group
of us had shawarma and falafel, the noise had become the bleat
of military jeep horns, the squeal of a car and a voice shouting
through a bullhorn – border police or IDF, I don't remember
which. As the training went on, there was noise and flashing
lights outside – but it wasn't real for me somehow because I
was inside this building with these people. Everyone extending
theories into the air.

The scariest thing for non-Jewish Americans in talking about
Palestinian self-determination is the fear of being or sounding
anti-Semitic. The people of Israel are suffering and Jewish
people have a long history of oppression. We still have some
responsibility for that, but I think it's important to draw a firm

distinction between the policies of Israel as a state, and Jewish people. That's kind of a no-brainer, but there is very strong pressure to conflate the two. I try to ask myself, whose interest does it serve to identify Israeli policy with all Jewish people?

Anyway, this kind of stuff I just think about all the time and my ideas evolve. I'm really new to talking about Israel-Palestine, so I don't always know the political implications of my words.

Reading from her notebook.

Notes from Training:
When Talking – no hearsay. Call hospitals and official sources. Use quotes. Don't appear to judge rightness or wrongness. Non-Violence – Don't touch those we're confronting. Don't run. Carry nothing that could be used as a weapon. No self-initiating actions.

January 26th.

Travel from Beit Sahour to Jerusalem.

January 27th.

An attack in Gaza the night before last killed fourteen and injured around thirty.

The West Bank and Gaza are under extremely strict curfew until after the election tomorrow. You are not allowed to leave your house at all. Not for food. Nothing. I am still in Jerusalem aiming to get to Rafah to join the other internationals trying to prevent the demolition of civilian homes.

I am relatively sheltered here. Walking around with Palestinians I wait while they are stopped to show ID. Blue stars of David are spray-painted on doors in the Arab section of the old city. I have never seen that symbol used in quite that way. I am used to seeing the *cross* used in a colonialist way. I know this is something I can't really understand, right now. The reality of curfew, of the checkpoints. I'm sort of embarrassed about how long it takes me to realize in my gut that people live like this . . .

Reading from her notebook.

At 10pm, I travel to Rafah. Jehan met the cab. Soldiers at bus stations. Bombed market in Gaza City. Children grab my ass, throw garbage at my head, scream, 'What's your name?'

Writing in her notebook.

Sleep in tent. Gunshot through tent. Start smoking.

January 31st.

Today I decided to follow Joe's lead and write in every spare crack of time in every day. I always regret the blank space in my journal from Russia. Here it is different. I am older and the world does not revolve around me. We are in Jehan's brother's apartment in Khan Younis.

The neighborhoods that have asked us for some form of presence are Yibna, Tel El Sultan, Hi Salam, Brazil, Block J, Zorob, and Block O.

There is some visible class difference between this building in Khan Younis and, say, Brazil or Block J. There are toys for the children. A table. But this apartment – with blank walls and birds weaving in and out of the windows – would be symptomatic of nearly crushing poverty in the United States.

There is greenery here. Some trees and grassy places – maybe it is shielded a little by Rafah which is razed and bullet-riddled and bare. Jehan's uncle came to sit with us. He told us that there was a peaceful time in the late '70s and early '80s. 'We build their buildings. We work in the factory.' He says it is the leaders that make war.

Writing in her journal.

Today. Visits to –
Gaza, re: Nursing
UN
Children's Parliament
Women's group.

We need to make:
One beautiful banner in Arabic and English.

February 1st.

After we'd helped the water people do more repairs we had gone to look for banner fabric. Jehan found Will and me waiting to pay the man for 30 meters of white cotton. She told us someone had been killed at the Rafah/Egypt border. We met up at the apartment and rode in a strangely Californian SUV past the cemetery to the Palestinian side of the border. A swarm of people waited there. We were given a stretcher and ushered into an office. People talked for a while and then we went out – each of us with a handle.

We started into the field: five internationals plus Jehan. Jenny spoke over the bullhorn saying, 'Do not shoot. We are unarmed civilians,' naming the countries we came from and letting the IDF know our intention to retrieve this man's body.

The first response from the IDF was shouting, 'Go back.' Then they shot about 20 meters in front of us.

As we continued to walk in the direction of the body – the shots shifted – hitting the ground two to four meters in front of us. We also heard two high-pitched, whistling shots above our heads. We stopped and Jenny requested to talk to the commanding officer.

A white truck with a blue light rolled up and the person in the truck spoke over the loudspeaker. Told us to leave. Stated, 'You'll get the body later.'

The white truck cruised away.

Then a tank and a bulldozer emerged from the IDF side of the checkpoint and proceeded toward the olive grove. They began moving dirt between us and the olive grove. Smoke blew.

They created a mound of dirt and shot repeatedly into it.

This is my very poor drawing of the dead body we just carried. He had a big white hand poised in the air off the stretcher as if doing the crawl or throwing a baseball.

Had a dream about falling, falling to my death off of something dusty and smooth and crumbling like the cliffs in Utah, but I kept holding on, and when each new foothold or handle of rock broke, I reached out as I fell and grabbed a new one. I didn't have time to think about anything – just react as if I was playing an adrenaline-filled video game. And I heard, 'I can't die, I can't die,' again and again in my head. Seems somehow positive compared to the dreams I used to have of tumbling, thinking, 'This is it, I'm going to die.'

Reading from her notebook.

February 4th.

In Dr Samir's garden.

Fig tree with small buds. Dill, lettuce, garlic.
White plastic chairs, deflated soccer ball, blanket drying on
a line.
Patchy lawn, long shadows.
Two bulldozers, tanks.

I went to the kitchen and stayed two hours. The tank stayed
too, so no work, no school.

A soldier came with a sledgehammer.
The tank started firing – the family were watching *Tom &
Jerry* in the kitchen.
I played with the children to distract them.

Dr Samir says, 'Before intifada – no tanks, no bulldozers, no
gunshots, no noise.
After intifada, daily. Gunshots daily.
I have no gun in my house, nothing.
30 years collecting money for house.
We also afraid no other place to go, three hours they can
destroy house.
I look at my garden. I ask myself, "This year will you eat from
these trees like other years?" – I trust in my god – so no
problem.'

February 6th.

I rode on the bulldozer as it repaired the road throughout the day. Jenny and Will held a banner and spoke through the megaphone for us. A tank stayed present throughout the action. And at some point a jeep arrived. This frightened me because I know at least one person was shot by soldiers in a green jeep.

Some youths – maybe three – came out toward the banner, and then soldiers got out of the jeep and shot toward the internationals. Jehan found bits of shrapnel later in her shoes.

Rafah
Ghost homes
Glow-in-the-dark stars in teenagers' bedrooms
Tumbling of concrete
Constant anonymous night-vision telescope.

February 7th.

I have been in Palestine for two weeks and one hour now, and I still have very few words to describe what I see. I don't know if many of the children here have ever existed without tank-shell holes in their walls. I think even the smallest of these children understand that life is not like this everywhere. They love to get me to practise my limited Arabic. Today I tried to learn to say, 'Bush is a tool', but I don't think it translated quite right. But anyway, there are eight-year-olds here more aware of the workings of the global power structure than I was just a few years ago – at least regarding Israel.

Nothing could have prepared me for the reality of the situation here. You just can't imagine it unless you see it. And even then your experience is not at all the reality: what with the difficulties the Israeli army would face if they shot an unarmed US citizen, the fact that I have money to buy water when the army destroys wells, and of course, the fact that I have the option of leaving. I am allowed to see the ocean.

If I feel outrage at entering briefly into the world in which these children exist, I wonder how it would be for them to arrive in my world. Once you have seen the ocean and lived in a silent place where water is taken for granted and not stolen in the night by bulldozers, spent an evening when you didn't wonder if the walls of your home might suddenly fall inward, aren't surrounded by towers, tanks, and now a giant metal wall, I wonder if you can forgive the world for all the years spent existing – just existing – in resistance to the constant attempt to erase you from your home. That is something I wonder about these children. I wonder what would happen if they really knew.

I am in Rafah. A city of 140,000 people, 60% of whom are refugees – many twice or three times over. Currently, the Israeli army is building a twelve-meter-high wall between Rafah and the border. 602 homes have been completely bulldozed and the number partially destroyed is greater.

Today, as I walked on top of the rubble, Egyptian soldiers called to me from the other side of the border: 'Go! Go!' because a tank was coming. And then waving and 'What's your name?' Something disturbing about this friendly curiosity. To some degree, we are all kids curious about other kids. Egyptian kids shouting at strange women wandering into the path of tanks. Palestinian kids shot from the tanks when they peek out from behind walls to see what's going on. International kids standing in front of tanks with banners. Israeli kids in the tanks – occasionally shouting, occasionally waving – many forced to be here, many just aggressive, anonymously shooting into the houses as we wander away.

In addition to tanks, there are more IDF towers than I can count. Some just army-green metal, others these strange spiral staircases draped in some kind of netting. A new one went up the other day in the time it took us to do laundry and cross town twice to hang banners. And nowhere invulnerable to Apache helicopters or the cameras of invisible drones we hear buzzing over the city for hours at a time.

We've been wavering between five and six of us internationals. There are requests for constant nighttime presence at a well on the outskirts of Rafah since the two largest wells were destroyed last week, but after about 10pm it is very difficult to move because the Israeli army treats anyone in the streets as resistance and shoots at them. So clearly we are too few.

I went to a rally a few days ago in Khan Younis in solidarity with the people of Iraq. Many analogies were made about the continuing suffering of the Palestinian people and the upcoming occupation of Iraq by the United States – not the war itself, but the certain aftermath of the war.

People here watch the media, and they told me again today that there have been large protests in the United States and 'problems for the government' in the UK. So now I don't feel like a complete Pollyanna when I tell people that not everyone in the United States supports the policies of our government.

I'm just beginning to learn from what I expect to be a very intense tutelage in the ability of people to organize against all odds, and to resist against all odds.

I knew a few years ago what the unbearable lightness was, before I read the book. The lightness – between life and death, there are no dimensions at all. There are no rulers or mile-markers. It's just a shrug – the difference between Hitler and my mother, the difference between Whitney Houston and a Russian mother watching her son fall through the sidewalk and boil to death. There are no rules. There is no fairness. There are no guarantees. No warranties on anything. It's all just a shrug, the difference between ecstasy and misery is just a shrug. And with that enormous shrug there, the shrug between being and not being – how could I be a poet? How could I believe in a truth?

And I knew, back then, that the shrug would happen at the end of my life – I knew. And I thought, so who cares? If my whole life is going to amount to one shrug and a shake of the head, who cares if it comes in eighty years or at 8pm? Who cares?

Now, I know who cares. I know if I die at 11.15pm or at 97 years – I know. And I know it's me. That's my job.

Reading from her notebook.

February 11th.

Tufah Checkpoint.
Women and kids on right, men on left, ID passes in their hands.
The women with babies and buckets – all middle-aged.

At 2pm they said the checkpoint would open.
2.40pm – it opens.

Six old men proceed, then the IDF announces only five at a time.
Then came five women with four children and a baby in arms.

A soldier runs forward, yelling.
The women kneel, stand up again, and return.

3pm – five or six men go through.
3.04pm – five more.

3.10pm – the group of women and children proceed again.
3.25pm – five men waiting.

February 20th.

Both of the major checkpoints are closed. This means that
Palestinians who want to go and register for their next quarter
at university can't. People can't get to their jobs; those who are
trapped on the other side can't get home; and internationals,
who have a meeting tomorrow in the West Bank, won't make
it. We could if we made serious use of our international white-
person privilege, but that would also mean some risk of arrest
and deportation, even though none of us have done anything
illegal.

I am staying put in Rafah for now, no plans to head north.
A lot of very nice Palestinians are looking after me. I have
a small flu bug and got some lemony drinks to cure me. Also,
the woman who keeps the key for the well where we still sleep
keeps asking about my mom – wants to make sure I'm calling
you.

She goes to the computer.

Checking e-mails.

Rachel,

I am very concerned for you. But I know most of this is not about you, but about the people, the families you are building solidarity with. I have worried a little, because it seems to me that it could be easy to be manipulated by one faction or another. For myself, I feel like I'm fighting a lifetime of indoctrination. Palestinians have really been invisible to me, but you are changing that.

In regards to Palestinian violence, I just abhor any violence. I understand that most are just trying feebly to defend themselves, but here, just the mention of suicide bombing puts up a wall.

There is a lot in my heart but I am having trouble with the words. Be safe, be well. Do you think about coming home? Because of war and all? I know probably not, but I hope you feel it would be okay if you did.

Mama.

She replies.

February 28th.

Mom,

I spent the evening and this morning with a family on the front line in Hi Salam – who fixed me dinner – and have cable TV. The two front rooms of their house are unusable because gunshots have been fired through the walls, so the whole family sleep in the parents' bedroom. I sleep on the floor next to the youngest daughter and we all share blankets. I helped the son with his English homework a little, and we all watched *Pet Sematary*, which is a horrifying movie. They all thought it was pretty funny how much trouble I had watching it. Friday is the holiday, and when I woke up they were watching *Gummi Bears* dubbed into Arabic. So I ate breakfast with them and sat there for a while and just enjoyed being in this big puddle of blankets with this family watching what for me seemed like Saturday morning cartoons.

Then I walked some way to Brazil Block, which is where the big family live, the one that has wholeheartedly adopted me. The other day, the grandmother gave me a lecture that involved a lot of blowing and pointing to her black shawl. I got Nidal to tell her that my mother would appreciate knowing that someone here was giving me a hard time about smoking turning my lungs black.

I am amazed at their strength in defending such a large degree of their humanity against the incredible horror occurring in their lives and against the constant presence of death. I think the word is dignity.

Of course, we burn out. Of course, it is overwhelming. Whenever I organize or participate in public protest I get really worried that it will just suck, be really small, embarrassing, and the media will laugh at us. Oftentimes it is really small and most of the time the media does laugh at us and of course it doesn't get coverage all over the world, but in some places the word 'Rafah' is mentioned outside of the Arab press. If the international media and our government are not going to tell us that we are effective, valuable, we have to do that for each other, and one way we can do that is by continuing our work, visibly.

I look forward to seeing more and more people willing to resist the direction the world is moving in: a direction where our personal experiences are irrelevant, that we are defective, that our communities are not important, that we are powerless, that the future is determined, and that the highest level of humanity is expressed through what we choose to buy at the mall.

Maybe you should try to get Dad to quit his neo-liberal job and become a Math teacher. Maybe you should try to get him to sabotage his neo-liberal job. Do you think he could accidentally dump a lot of dollars very cheaply into international markets? Okay. Sorry. I love you guys. Take care of yourselves.

Writing in notebook.

Set up system for media work
Prepare paragraph for rally
Go to Block J and investigate home
Stay and work tonight
Call Dr Samir.

Checking e-mail.

Todd!

Reading e-mail.

Hey you!

Keep up the strength. It is much needed in this world. You really make me want to go there.

She replies.

Holy shit, Todd – come here! The work we do needs people who know how to support this community, not just start our own separate 'international solidarity show'. The people here are incredible.

Come here come here come here come here come here come here come here come here come here come here.

Writing in her notebook.

Call Gili for talk with Alice
Plan for Women's Day
Saturday am – choose new house.

At the computer.

March 1st.

10.30am – three internationals joined four men at the El Iskan water well. It provides 25% of Rafah's water supply.

Workers at the well reported being fired upon on Thursday.

Despite guarantees of safety and presence of banners and megaphones, activists and workers were fired on several times over a period of one hour, close enough to spray debris in their faces.

For information about the report and other issues related to the destruction of civilian water supplies in Rafah, please contact Rachel.

Writing in her notebook.

We need:
Battery-charged striplights
Megaphone
Lamps
Fabric
Envelopes.

Checking e-mail.

Dad . . .

She reads.

Rachel,

I find writing to you hard, but not thinking about you impossible. So I don't write, but I do bore my friends at lunch, giving vent to my fear. I am afraid for you, and I think I have reason to be. But I'm also proud of you – very proud. But as Don Remfert says: I'd just as soon be proud of somebody else's daughter. That's how fathers are: we're hard-wired not to want our children, no matter how old they are, no matter how brave they are, and no matter how much good they are doing, to be subject to so much threat or even to witness so much suffering. You may say (have said) that it is wrong for me to stick my head in the sand; but I say I am only trying to (or just wishing

I could) stick your head in the sand – and that's different. Hard-wired. Can't be changed on that aspect of the issue.

She replies.

Hi Papa,

I feel like sometimes I spend all my time propagandizing Mom, and assuming that she'll pass stuff on to you, so you get neglected. Don't worry about me too much, right now I am most concerned that we are not being effective. I still don't feel particularly at risk.

I am trying to figure out what I'm going to do when I leave here.

One of the core members of our group has to leave tomorrow, and watching her say goodbye is making me realize how difficult it will be. People here can't leave, so that complicates things. They are also pretty matter-of-fact about whether or not they will be alive when we come back here. I really don't want to live with a lot of guilt about this place – being able to come and go so easily. I know I should try and link up with the family in France, but I think that I'm not going to do that. I would just be angry, and not much fun to be around. It seems like a transition into too much opulence right now – I would feel a lot of class guilt the whole time.

Let me know if you have any ideas about what I should do with the rest of my life. If you want, you can write to me as if I was on vacation at a camp on Hawaii learning to weave. One thing I do to make things easier here is to utterly retreat into fantasies that I am in a Hollywood movie, or a sitcom starring Michael J. Fox. So feel free to make something up and I'll be happy to play along.

I remember the morning I walked with Colin to Puget Pantry to get cigarettes and a few last-minute prizes for a bingo game at work. It was my last day as 'drop-ins coordinator' at Behavioral Health Resources – a community service for mental-health clients. We met once a week to develop social skills.

I convinced Colin to walk with me because Puget Pantry had 'The Who's Tommy Pinball'.

On the radio the announcers were talking about giving blood.

I asked the man behind the counter what happened.

'Two towers. Someone bomb.'

'Someone bombed the World Trade Center?'

'Airplanes.'

Colin and I sat on the sidewalk beneath the payphone. We thought it might be World War III. I called my dad.

I figured if it was World War III, being 'drop-ins coordinator' was a damn fine situation to go out in.

I took the clients out
in the company car
for insurance reasons today
to Dairy Queen

and purchased them all dip cones and French Fries
with company cash
not my own
for ethical reasons

and when they offered me a fry
I did not accept it
also for ethical reasons
but instead ate only
ketchup and fire sauce with my finger

and they confessed
one by one that their voices were accusing me of hypocrisy
so I initiated a long talk about their trust issues
and they each cried a little
and Jim lost his appetite

so we processed that while the butterscotch shell wilted off his
dip cone
and he cried some more
and called me a hairy little bitch sabotaging his ice-cream day
so I refocused him
on his own anxiety

and asked if he wanted to go back to the hospital
and he said
fucking hell
no
I do not and

I said I hear that you're feeling angry
but you'll have to use appropriate social skills and language
or there won't be anymore Dairy Queen

and then the clients got very escalated
and asked me just what exactly I was threatening to do
to Dairy Queen
You power drunk little
overeducated slut

and I put everyone on timeout
to practice their deep breathing
and then everybody's dip cones melted
and the cones got all soggy
and I think April tried to kick me in the shin beneath the table.

By the time timeout was over
the surface of our table was completely decompensated
and Jim was whispering to himself
between deep breaths
and I gently asked if he was responding
to internal stimuli

and he made an obscene gesture with his right hand
and spit in my reservoir of ketchup and fire sauce
and then the Dairy Queen guy saw our table and
asked us to leave.

On the ride back in the company car
the clients asked me

how can we maintain a healthy and goal-directed outlook on
our lives
when the very people who are paid to empower
and advocate for us
allow our dip cones to melt

and make veiled threats against Dairy Queen

and sometimes appear to intentionally make us cry?

and I said
have you noticed those lovely clouds over there
on the horizon all rosy and backlit by the sun?
why don't we all focus on the rosy clouds and practice our
relaxation skills?

and they said, yes, we have
noticed
back in the Dairy Queen
when you made us breathe
and please desist from using the word *we* as a transparent and
superficial attempt
to transcend the client/counselor relationship and

persuade us to
trust your
bony ass

and I said
what's that like for you
and they said
shut it – okay.
hippie?
our voices are telling us you
suck ass
and really need to get laid

and I bracketed my personal feelings and pulled over
and said
you are never going to eat at Dairy Queen again
I swear it on my mother's grave.
and we drove on
in silence.

Hey
they said
since
you are obviously cracking and made an atrocious breach of
professionalism
do you think
today can be
Mexico day?

and I said
what?

and they said
what?

and I said
what did you just ask me?

and they all stared at me in the rearview mirror
and that's when I realized
nobody
said
anything
at all

but April winked
before I flicked my eyes back to the road
and Kelly said
we've got the car

and I said
yeah.
I got the gas card too.

And Jim said
Sorry your mom's dead
And I said
that's okay Jim
we all deal with loss throughout our lives
and
he said
don't push it

and we sang a lot of Beatles songs
in Oregon
and Good-bye Ruby Tuesday
728 times in California
and The Dead
on the border
and all the voices joined in
on the harmony
for Bobby and Phil.

I look at things the wrong way. I know I do. I know how it
feels not to be normal, though. I don't know how it feels to
have voices or to sleep in those beds with the white knitted
blankets. But yeah, those times when you just know the whole
world is out there, patting their stomachs and saying, 'God
bless us, every one.' And you're inside with the box of blue
plastic gloves for cooking and the no-self-harm contracts and
the antibacterial hand-cleanser.

How you survive in a nonexistent place.

Make a list:
God
breakfast cereal
the prophet Mohammed
play bus
weapons of mass destruction
corner grocery
tawdry affair
Mel Gibson
sandstorm
venereal disease
malnutrition
proxy government
water contamination

Choices:
1. Go back to Olympia.
Finish school. Talk or presentations about Gaza. Clean out my stuff from Sarah's garage.

2. Go to Egypt or Dubai for a year.
Earn money, learn Arabic. Come back to Palestine.

3. Go to Sweden for one month.
Potentially horrible. Go broke.

4. Try to stay in Rafah.
Money? Productivity?

5. Travel elsewhere.

I think my soul is nomadic. I've always turned my head a little to listen out of one ear to the people speaking in Spanish behind me on the bus. I've always stared upward at airplanes cutting white paths through the sky and wondered where they're going. I've always been jealous of migratory birds.

In a year or two, or maybe next winter, I'll go to South America.

I will smile across the water at the Olympics. When I leave, I'll ride up over the rises and dips of that road that I've been riding over all my life, through the cedars and past the barn. I'll lean out the window when I pass my old high school and scream, 'Ha Ha Ha! Fuck You! Fuck You!' just for old times' sake. I'll get on Highway 101 and when it reaches I-5, I'll either go north towards the airport or south towards Mexico.

When I leave, I'll leave laughing. I'll come back to see my mother and my college friends and to swim naked in Puget Sound at night. And I won't be afraid to come back, like I've always been afraid before. I'll cry, but I'll be smiling, and I'll hug my mom.

She goes to the computer.

March 9th.

Today's Demo.
At least ten greenhouses destroyed. Cucumbers, peas, olives, tomatoes.
Quiet area. 300 people dependent on farms to live.
150-200 men arrested.
Shot around them. Beat them. Six people in hospital.

They don't understand what has happened.

March 13th, 9pm.

Intensive care unit – 12-year-old girl shot from tower in school near Nasser hospital.

11pm – shooting behind West Camp.
Came from settlement into main market – two or three Apaches.

Evacuated apartment building – eight families.

Shot inside hospital – three injured – nurses.

6am – houses demolished.

41 injured.

Mom.

I have bad nightmares about tanks and bulldozers outside our house, and you and me inside. Sometimes the adrenaline acts as an anesthetic for weeks – and then at night it just hits me again a little bit of the reality of the situation. I am really scared for the people here. Yesterday I watched a father lead his two tiny children holding his hand out into the sight of tanks and a sniper tower and bulldozers because he thought his house was going to be exploded.

It was our mistake in translation that made him think this, although I'm sure it is only a matter of time. In fact, the Israeli army was in the process of detonating an explosive in the ground nearby. This is in the area where Sunday about 150 men were rounded up outside the settlement with gunfire over their heads, while tanks and bulldozers destroyed twenty-five greenhouses – the livelihoods of three hundred people. To think that this man felt it was less of a risk to walk out in view of the tanks with his kids than to stay in his house. I was really scared that they were all going to be shot, and I tried to stand between them and the tank. This happens every day, but this father walking out with his two little kids just looking very sad, happened to get my attention more at this particular moment, probably because I felt like it was our translation problems that made him leave.

I thought a lot about what you said about Palestinian violence not helping the situation. 60,000 people from Rafah worked in Israel two years ago. Now only 600 can go there for jobs. Of these 600, many have moved, because the three checkpoints make a 40-minute drive into a 12-hour or impassable journey.

Sources of economic growth are all completely destroyed – the airport (runways demolished, totally closed); the border for trade with Egypt (now with a sniper tower in the middle of the crossing); access to the ocean (completely cut off in the last two years).

There used to be a middle class here – recently. We get reports that in the past, Gazan flower shipments to Europe were delayed for two weeks for security inspections. You can imagine the value of two-week-old cut flowers, so that market dried up. And then the bulldozers come and take out vegetable farms and gardens. What is left for people? Tell me if you can think of anything. I can't.

So when someone says that any act of Palestinian violence justifies Israel's actions not only do I question that logic in light of international law and the right of people to legitimate armed struggle in defence of their land and their families; not only do I question that logic in light of the fourth Geneva Convention which prohibits collective punishment, prohibits the transfer of an occupying country's population into an occupied area, prohibits the expropriation of water resources and the destruction of civilian infrastructure such as farms; not only do I question that logic in light of the notion that fifty-year-old Russian guns and homemade explosives can have any impact on the activities of one of the world's largest militaries, backed by the world's only superpower, I also question that logic on the basis of common sense.

If any of us had our lives and welfare completely strangled and lived with children in a shrinking place where we knew that soldiers and tanks and bulldozers could come for us at any moment, with no means of economic survival and our houses demolished; if they came and destroyed all the greenhouses that we'd been cultivating for the last however long do you not think, in a similar situation, most people would defend themselves as best they could?

You asked me about non-violent resistance, and I mentioned the first intifada. The vast majority of Palestinians right now, as far as I can tell, are engaging in Gandhian non-violent resistance. Who do you think I'm staying with, in houses that are going to be demolished amid gunfire? Who do you think are staffing the human-rights centers? What do you think this Palestinian-led movement is that I joined that engages in non-violent direct action? Who do you think these families are that I tell you about, who won't take any money from us even though they are very, very poor, and who say to us: 'We are not a hotel. We help you because we think maybe you will go and tell people in your country that you lived with Muslims. We think they will know that we are good people. We are quiet people. We just want peace'? Do you think I'm hanging out with Hamas fighters? These people are being shot at every day and they continue to go about their business as best they can in the sights of machine guns and rocket launchers. Isn't that basically the epitome of non-violent resistance?

When that explosive detonated yesterday it broke all the windows in the family's house. I was in the process of being served tea and playing with the two small babies.

I'm having a hard time right now. Just feel sick to my stomach from being doted on very sweetly, by people who are facing doom. I know that from the United States it all sounds like hyperbole. A lot of the time the kindness of the people here, coupled with the willful destruction of their lives, makes it seem unreal to me. I can't believe that something like this can happen in the world without a bigger outcry. It hurts me, again, like it has hurt me in the past, to witness how awful we can allow the world to be.

For a long time I've been operating from a certain core assumption that we are all essentially the same inside, and that our differences are by and large situational. That goes for everybody – Bush, Bin Laden, Tony Blair, me, you, Sarah, Chris, Dad, Gram, Palestinians, everybody of any particular religion. I know there is a good chance that this assumption actually is false. But it's convenient, because it always leads to questions about the way privilege shelters people from the consequences of their actions. It's also convenient because it leads to some level of forgiveness, whether justified or not.

It is my own selfishness and will to optimism that wants to believe that even people with a great deal of privilege don't just idly sit by and watch. What we are paying for here is truly evil. Maybe the general growing class imbalance in the world and consequent devastation of working people's lives is a bigger evil. Being here should make me more aware of what it means to be a farmer in Colombia, for example. Anyway, I'm rambling. Just want to tell my mom that I'm really scared, and questioning my fundamental belief in the goodness of human nature. This has to stop. I think it is a good idea for us all to drop everything and devote our lives to making this stop. I don't think it's an extremist thing to do any more. I still really want to dance around to Pat Benatar and have boyfriends and make comics for my co-workers. But I also want this to stop. Disbelief and horror is what I feel. Disappointment. I am disappointed that this is the base reality of our world and that we, in fact, participate in it. This is not at all what I asked for when I came into this world. This is not at all what the people here asked for when they came into this world. This is not what they are asking for now. This is not the world you and Dad wanted me to come into when you decided to have me. This is not what I meant when I was two and looked at Capitol Lake and said, 'This is the wide world and I'm coming to it.'

When I come back from Palestine I probably will have nightmares and constantly feel guilty for not being here, but I can channel that into more work. Coming here is one of the better things I've ever done.

I love you and Dad. Sorry for the diatribe.

A door opens.

Okay, some strange men are offering me some peas, so I need to eat and thank them.

She leaves.

From the TV set, a recording of the transcript of an eyewitness account by Tom Dale.

Rachel walked to place herself in between the home and the bulldozer. As the bulldozer turned towards them, it had about 20 metres or 10 seconds clear time directly with her in its view to see where she was. It continued toward her at some pace with a mound of earth building up in front of it. And as the mound of earth reached Rachel she obviously felt that in order to keep her balance, to keep her footing she had to climb on to this mound of earth to prevent being overwhelmed by it. When she did this it put her head and shoulders clearly above the top of the bulldozer blade and therefore clearly in the view of the bulldozer driver, so he knew absolutely that she was there.

She falls down the mound of earth and out of sight of the driver; so he has essentially pushed her forward down the mound of earth. And then she starts to slide and then you see one then both of her feet disappear and he simply continued until she was, or the place where she had been, was directly beneath the cockpit of the bulldozer. They waited a few seconds then withdrew leaving his scoop on the ground. Only later when it was much clear of her body did it raise its scoop.

I ran for an ambulance, she was gasping and her face was covered in blood from a gash cutting her face from lip to cheek. She was showing signs of brain haemorrhaging. She died in the ambulance a few minutes later.

Rachel Corrie

was killed on March 16th, 2003.

A video of Rachel Corrie, aged ten, appears on the screen.
This was recorded at her school's Fifth Grade Press
Conference on World Hunger

'I'm here for other children.
I'm here because I care.
I'm here because children everywhere are suffering and
because forty thousand people die each day from hunger.
I'm here because those people are mostly children.
We have got to understand that the poor are all around us and
we are ignoring them.
We have got to understand that these deaths are preventable.
We have got to understand that people in Third World
countries think and care and smile and cry just like us.
We have got to understand that they dream our dreams and we
dream theirs.
We have got to understand that they are us. We are them.
My dream is to stop hunger by the year 2000.
My dream is to give the poor a chance.
My dream is to save the forty thousand people who die each day.
My dream can and will come true if we all look into the future
and see the light that shines there.
If we ignore hunger, that light will go out.
If we all help and work together, it will grow and burn free
with the potential of tomorrow.'

An Afterword

LET ME FIGHT MY MONSTERS

By Katharine Viner

There is a particular entry in Rachel Corrie's diary, probably
written sometime in 1999, four years before she was killed
by an Israeli bulldozer in the Gaza Strip trying to prevent the
demolition of Palestinian homes. She is aged nineteen or twenty.
"Had a dream about falling, falling to my death off something
dusty and smooth and crumbling like the cliffs in Utah," she
writes, "but I kept holding on, and when each foothold or
handle of rock broke I reached out as I fell and grabbed a new
one. I didn't have time to think about anything—just react as
if I was playing an adrenaline-filled video game. And I heard,
'I can't die, I can' t die,' again and again in my head."

Last year, I was asked by the Royal Court Theatre to edit
the writings of Rachel Corrie into a drama with Alan Rickman,
who was also directing. I had read the powerful e-mails she
sent home from Gaza, serialized in G2 in the days after her
death, and I'd read eyewitness accounts on the internet. But
I didn't know that Rachel's early writing—before she even
thought of traveling to the Middle East, from her days as a
schoolgirl, through college, to life working at a mental-health
center in her hometown of Olympia, Washington—would be
similarly fascinating, and contain such elements of chilling
prescience. Nor did I have a sense of the kind of person
Rachel Corrie was: a messy, skinny, Dali-loving, list-making
chain-smoker, with a passion for the music of Pat Benatar.
I discovered all that later.

Rachel was killed, aged twenty-three, on March 16, 2003,
by a Caterpillar D-9 bulldozer, a vehicle especially built to
demolish houses. Three decades before, her father had driven
bulldozers in Vietnam for the U.S. army. Her death was the

first of a string of killings of westerners in Gaza in spring 2003, as the war was taking place in Iraq—Briton Tom Hurndall, twenty-two, was shot on April 11, and another Briton, cameraman James Miller, thirty-four, was shot on May 16. She and Hurndall were activists in the International Solidarity Movement (ISM), an organization set up "to support Palestinian nonviolent resistance to Israel's military occupation." Rachel was killed only two days before the start of the assault on Baghdad while the world was mostly looking elsewhere.

She became a martyr to the Palestinians, a victim of their intifada who had stood up to the mighty Israeli army. Edward Said praised her actions as "heroic and dignified at the same time." But many Israelis considered her at best naive, interfering in a situation she didn't understand. And to some Americans she was a traitor. Websites blared: "she should burn in hell for an eternity"; "good riddance to bad rubbish"; "I'm thankful she died."

Those close to Rachel would rather she had not become famous for being the blond American girl who got killed. As her ex-boyfriend, Colin Reese, said in the documentary *Death of an Idealist*: "The person that I knew has been summed up as a bullet point . . . Everything that Rachel was, every brilliant idea she had, every art project she did, it doesn't matter, because she has become her death."

In developing this piece of theatre, we wanted to uncover the young woman behind the political symbol, beyond her death. As Alan Rickman, whose idea it was to turn Rachel's work into drama, says: "We were never going to paint Rachel as a golden saint or sentimentalize her, but we also needed to face the fact that she'd been demonized. We wanted to present a balanced portrait." We hoped to find out what made Rachel Corrie different from the stereotype of today's consumerist, depoliticized youth. Having received permission from Rachel's parents to shape her words into drama, we were sent an enormous package—184 pages of her writing, most of which had not been seen before.

The material revealed a woman who was both ordinary and extraordinary: writing poems about her cat, her friends, her grandmother, the wind, but, also, from a strikingly young age, engaging passionately with the world, trying to find her place in it. The earliest material we have is political—at age ten, Rachel wrote a poem about how "children everywhere are suffering" and how she wished to "stop hunger by the year 2000." Her juvenilia shows, as Rickman says, that she "already knew what language was. She was witty, a story-teller, she had flights of fancy." It also shows a rather sweet seriousness, and an insight into the wider world and her place in it. At age twelve, she writes, "I guess I've grown up a little. It's all relative anyway—nine years is as long as forty years depending on how long you've lived."

In her teens, Rachel started to write about the "fire in my belly" that was to become a recurring theme. She visited Russia, a trip that opened her eyes to the rest of the world—she found it "flawed, dirty, broken and gorgeous." And she engaged in a striking way with her parents, with writing that beautifully expresses ordinary anxieties about safety and free-dom, which become particularly poignant in light of Rachel's violent death. At age nineteen she wrote to her mother, "I know I scare you . . . But I want to write and I want to see. And what would I write about if I only stayed within the doll's house, the flower-world I grew up in? . . . I love you but I'm growing out of what you gave me . . . Let me fight my monsters. I love you. You made me. You made me."

She stewed, in typical late-teens fashion, about her future, and wrote about men and sex, from falling "in love with someone who is perpetually leaving you . . . and tells all stories as if they are blues songs" to bumping into an ex-boyfriend with his "hoochie-ass" new lover. Her wit was of the sardonic kind, and is one of the main things her friends remember about her.

Rachel's political evolution gathered pace in her early twenties. She went to Evergreen State College, a famously liberal university in Olympia, itself a famously liberal town. She began railing against how "the highest level of humanity is expressed through what we choose to buy at the mall." After September 11, she became involved in community activism, organizing a peace march, but questioned the wider relevance of what she was doing: "People [are] offering them-selves as human shields in Palestine and I [am] spending all of my time making dove costumes and giant puppets." When she finally decided that she wanted to go to the Middle East, she explained her reason quite specifically: "I've had this underlying need to go to a place and meet people who are on the other end of the portion of my tax money that goes to fund the U.S. and other militaries."

When Rachel arrived in Rafah in the Gaza Strip, as Rickman says, "the rhythm of the writing changes dramatically. She has less time to consider but you can feel the growing fear." The Gaza dispatches are hard-hitting and intense, representing a profound experience. On arrival in Jerusalem she was shocked to see the Star of David spray-painted onto doors in the Arab section of the old city: "I have never seen the symbol used in quite that way . . . I am used to seeing the cross used in a colonialist way." In Gaza, she carried the body of a dead man on a stretcher while the Israeli army shot in front of her, but mostly her activism involved protection: staying overnight in the homes of families on the frontline to stop their demolition, standing in front of water workers at a well in Rafah as they came under fire "close enough to spray debris in their faces." (Before her death, Rachel believed, as did many activists, that her "international white person privilege" would keep her relatively safe.) Witnessing the occupation in action inspired in Rachel her strongest writing in her last days—her rage and bafflement at what she saw led to work of astonishing and cumulative power.

But the quantity of the material left us with a series of questions. How much of Rachel's life before she went to Gaza should we include? And should we quote other people? The trend in political theatre, from David Hare's *Permanent Way* to Victoria Brittain and Gillian Slovo's *Guantanamo*, is journalistic: the use of testimony, of interviews and on-the-record material rather than invention. But for us there could be no re-interviewing to fill in the gaps. We had a finite amount of words to work with, as Rachel was dead. I was very keen to use some of the e-mails that Rachel's parents, Cindy and Craig, sent to their daughter while she was in Gaza. They are full of the kind of worries any parent might have if their child was in a dangerous situation, but because Rachel never came home, they have a devastating poignancy. Two weeks before her daughter's death, Cindy e-mailed

Rachel: "There is a lot in my heart but I am having trouble with the words. Be safe, be well. Do you think about coming home? Because of the war and all? I know probably not, but I hope you feel it would be OK if you did."

And what about the voices of Rachel's friends? I interviewed many fellow ISM activists, most of whom have been deported from Israel since her death. We watched tapes of two of the moving memorial services: one in Gaza, which was shot at by the Israeli army, another in Olympia. We viewed documentaries on the subject, most notably Sandra Jordan's powerful *Killing Zone*, and considered using video grabs. But in the end the power of Rachel's writing meant that, apart from a few short passages quoting her parents and an eyewitness report of her death, her words were strong enough to stand alone.

The challenge, then, was trying to construct a piece of theatre from fragments of journals, letters and e-mails, none of which was written with performance in mind. It helped, as Rickman says, that Rachel's writing "has a kind of theatricality. The images jump off the page." As the process went on, the difference between my usual job, journalism, and theatre, became obvious: stagecraft is what makes theatre what it is, and there was no point creating scenes that read well on the page if the actor playing Rachel, Megan Dodds, could not perform them.

We've tried to do justice to the whole of Rachel: neither saint nor traitor, both serious and funny, messy and talented, devastatingly prescient and human and whole. Or, in her own words, "scattered and deviant and too loud." We chose Rachel's words rather than those of the thousands of Palestinian or Israeli victims because of the quality and accessibility of the writing. As Rickman says, "The activist part of her life is absolutely matched by the imaginative part of her life. I've no doubt at all that had she lived, there would have been novels and plays pouring out of her." The tragedy is that we'll hear no more from Rachel Corrie.

Previously published in the Guardian *(London) April 8, 2005.*